Why the Moon Is Ivory

A Vietnamese Folktale
Retold by John Manos
Illustrated by
Cheryl Kirk Noll

Characters

Narrator

Jade Emperor

Queen Mother of the West

Sister Sun

Sister Moon

Winter Carriers   Summer Carriers

Rigby®
A Harcourt Achieve Imprint

www.Rigby.com
1-800-531-5015

Literacy by Design Leveled Readers: *Why the Moon Is Ivory*

ISBN-13: 978-1-4189-3904-5
ISBN-10: 1-4189-3904-8

Printed in China
5 6 7 8 0940 14 13 12 11 10

Contents

Act I
Scene 1

Narrator: Long ago when Earth was brand new, Jade Emperor ruled the skies and the weather. He sat on his great, golden throne that was carved with dragons and studied the people and animals of Earth. Beside him sat his kind and wise wife, Queen Mother of the West.

Jade Emperor: The world is a wonderful place, full of many marvelous things, but the people of Earth can barely see one another. They have only the dim gleam from the stars to guide them.

Queen Mother of the West: I also notice that their crops grow poorly in the darkness, and many families go hungry. Don't you hear the children crying for food and the parents sighing in sadness because they cannot feed their children?

Jade Emperor: I have decided that they need light and warmth to be happy, so I will send Thunder Spirit to give them flashes of light to help them see.

Queen Mother of the West: Thunder Spirit would frighten the people with the noise of his crashing thunder, and the heat of his lightning could harm them! How can you consider such an idea, especially when we have two beautiful, glowing daughters?

Narrator: Jade Emperor's deep laugh boomed from room to room like the rumbling roar of a huge drum.

Jade Emperor: Perhaps you're right—Thunder Spirit is a good messenger, and his blazing lightning helps guide the Rain Spirits to Earth. However, he is not gentle enough to watch over the people of Earth.

Queen Mother of the West: Then think hard, my husband, and figure out who will perform this very important task best.

Jade Emperor: In my opinion, the best one to ask is our oldest daughter, Sister Sun. She glows the most brightly of anyone, and her face shines more beautifully than the most magnificent star in the night sky.

Queen Mother of the West: Then let us send a messenger to bring Sister Sun to the throne room.

Act I
Scene 2

Narrator: After receiving her father's message, Sister Sun walked into the throne room, shining very brightly. Tall and slender, with a quiet voice and a serious manner, she was very aware of the responsibility of being Jade Emperor's oldest child. Sister Sun bowed respectfully to her father and waited to hear what he wanted.

Jade Emperor: My shining daughter, look down upon Earth and see its people as they are starving and stumbling in the dimness. I would like you to watch over them every day, turning your beautiful, golden face toward them to provide them with light and warmth.

Sister Sun: I'll polish my jewelry and my golden chair, and I'll wash my face until I'm the brightest light in the sky. I'll gladly provide warmth and comfort to all of the people. Thank you for your trust in me, my father.

Queen Mother of the West: My child, you will also help the people to know the seasons, showing them when to plant their rice fields and when to harvest their crops.

Jade Emperor: To help you with this task, I am giving you two teams of carriers to lift your chair and carry it across the sky.

Narrator: Into the throne room marched two sets of men, each group dressed exactly alike. The first group was made up of four young, strong men, with shining black hair and powerful muscles. The second was made up of four old men, with gray beards and backs bent with age.

Winter Carriers: Because we are young and strong, we will carry your shining chair swiftly across the sky from East to West, making the days short.

Jade Emperor: The short days will allow the people of Earth to know that it is winter and that it is time for them to rest from their work of planting and harvesting crops.

Summer Carriers: Because we are old and weak, we will rise early and our pace will be very slow. However, when we carry your shining chair across the sky from East to West, the days will be very long.

Queen Mother of the West: These summer carriers will give the people long, warm summer days when they can work on their farms and store food away for the winter.

Sister Sun: My father and my mother, I promise to care lovingly for the people of Earth, showing them season after season until the end of time.

Act II

Scene 1

Narrator: Day after day, Sister Sun and her brilliant golden chair were lifted across the sky from East to West by her carriers. In the summer the trip was slow, and in the winter it was swift. Therefore, the people of Earth knew when it was time to grow crops outside and when it was time to rest inside.

Jade Emperor: It makes my heart joyful to see how happy the people of Earth are as they work in their fields under the glow of Sister Sun!

Queen Mother of the West: Yes, Sister Sun's warmth and light are making the people's crops grow, and the people are very pleased. But this happens only during the days, when Sister Sun's face shines upon them.

Jade Emperor: What do you mean by that, my wife?

Queen Mother of the West: At night the world is completely dark. Can't you hear the children crying for their parents in the darkness? Don't you hear the worry in the parents' voices as they search for their lost children?

Narrator: Jade Emperor again studied Earth, and he listened carefully to the sound of the people crying out to one another in the night.

Jade Emperor: Why didn't I realize that the people need to be watched over at night as well as during the day? I have another daughter whose beauty is as great as Sister Sun's, so send for Sister Moon!

Narrator: When she heard her father's deep voice calling for her, Sister Moon rushed to him, bursting breathlessly into the throne room. She was filled with excitement, and her laughter sounded like the ringing of tiny silver bells.

Jade Emperor: My daughter, there is something that I would like you to do. You know how carefully your older sister watches over the people on Earth each day, lighting their way and warming their faces. We would like you to care for them during the night.

Sister Moon: This is the best news ever! Just let me polish my jewelry and light the lamps in the windows of my silver coach, and tonight I'll show everyone just how beautiful I am!

Queen Mother of the West: Wait and listen, my child. Instead of carriers, a great ox will pull your coach across the sky. This way, you will always move at the same speed, no matter how long or short the nights might be.

Sister Moon: I can't wait to polish my jewelry!

Jade Emperor: Well, she certainly is excited.

Queen Mother of the West: I just hope she is not too excited.

Act II
Scene 2

Narrator: At the end of that summer day, as Sister Sun traveled slowly down behind the western hills, the people left their fields to return to their homes for the night. But no sooner had the sun disappeared than it seemed to rise again in the East!

Sister Moon: I hope I'm not late! I can't believe how long it took me to polish all of my jewelry!

Narrator: Sister Moon rode proudly across the sky, her jewelry gleaming, and her bright face shining down on Earth. The people looked up and were amazed. Thinking it was day again, they went back into the rice fields and began working again.

Sister Moon: Look at all of the people who love my light! Tomorrow night and every night from now on, I'll give them as much warmth and light as my sister does! How happy they'll be!

Narrator: And so it continued, night after night. As soon as Sister Sun climbed down from her golden chair and her carriers rested, the great ox drove Sister Moon's silver coach into the sky. For the people of Earth, the days seemed endless, as if night never came. Without night they could not sleep, and they became very tired. Sister Moon was too excited by her job to realize that things were changing on Earth. However, Sister Sun noticed that something was terribly wrong.

Sister Sun: How odd this is! Each morning as we begin our journey across the sky, people are not coming out to their fields as they used to.

Summer Carriers: Where have all the people gone, Sister Sun?

Sister Sun: Many of the people are still asleep in their homes, and those who are outside look as though they are too tired to walk! Something is wrong, and I'm going to find out what it is.

Act II

Scene 3

Narrator: With her trusted Summer Carriers, Sister Sun came up with a plan.

Sister Sun: I know you have already carried me all day, Summer Carriers, but I need to learn what happens when my sister follows us into the sky. Tonight before we return to my palace to rest, please wait for a few minutes behind the western hills.

Summer Carriers: We will, Sister Sun.

Narrator: So Sister Sun waited to learn why the people no longer worked in their fields under her warm glow. She was furious when she saw what the problem was.

Sister Sun: Sister Moon, you are the reason the people are so tired! Every night when it should be dark and they should be sleeping in their homes, another day begins because of you!

Sister Moon: You're just jealous because the people like my beauty as much as they like yours!

Sister Sun: You are a proud and silly girl! You should think less about your beauty and more about the people who are your responsibility! Do the people on Earth look happy and healthy to you?

Narrator: Sister Moon had never noticed, but as she looked down, she saw that the people were exhausted. She lowered her head in shame and began to cry.

Sister Moon: I've been so foolish! I never meant to hurt any of the people on Earth. I am going to hide in my room forever!

Narrator: Seeing her younger sister's tears, Sister Sun felt pity for Sister Moon.

Sister Sun: I know you didn't mean to do any harm, my sister. You hope, like I do, to care for the people. Instead of hiding, let's talk with our parents and see what we can do.

Act III
Scene 1

Jade Emperor: What is the problem, my daughters? We could hear you arguing across the heavens, and now I see that Sister Moon has been crying!

Sister Moon: Oh, my father, I've made a huge mistake! When I let my face shine down on the people each night, all I do is keep them from getting any rest!

Sister Sun: The people of Earth no longer have cool nights in which to sleep. Instead they work in their fields until they are so tired they can barely move.

Sister Moon: My face is as bright as Sister Sun's, but I can't watch over the people if I turn my face away from them!

Queen Mother of the West: I think I can solve this problem. First, Sister Moon, I want you to take off your jewelry.

Sister Moon: Why? I've spent so much time polishing . . . !

Narrator: Queen Mother of the West held up her hand to stop Sister Moon's protest, and then gracefully unwrapped the pale silk scarf from her own neck.

Queen Mother of the West: I want you to wear this scarf as a veil, to soften the glow of your face.

Sister Moon: You mean I have to hide my lovely, polished jewelry and my beauty from the people! But why?

Queen Mother of the West: You will not be hiding your beauty. Your beauty will be a soft, ivory glow instead of the golden brightness of your sister's face. I am sure that the people will find you just as beautiful as your sister, whom they love.

Jade Emperor: I can see that you doubt your mother, Sister Moon. However, you must do as your mother says and watch over the people for at least one more night.

Act III
Scene 2

Narrator: Sister Moon bowed her head to show that she would obey, but she could not stop crying.

Sister Moon: OK, I'll do what you say and travel over Earth one last time, but then I'll go to my palace and stay there forever!

Queen Mother of the West: If that is your plan, then I will ride with you to see what this night is like.

Narrator: Queen Mother of the West climbed into Sister Moon's coach, but she wore a mask on her face so that the people would see only the pale glow of Sister Moon's face through the veil. As they began their journey across the night sky, they could hear cries of wonder and joy from Earth.

Sister Moon: What's that?

Queen Mother of the West: The people are singing about your beauty. Look at them celebrating—lighting fires and dancing—because your soft, ivory light is so beautiful in the night!

Sister Moon: Oh, I wish this night could last forever!

Narrator: As they made their way across the night sky, people everywhere looked up with happiness and sang to the ivory moon. At last Sister Moon and Queen Mother of the West returned to Jade Emperor's throne room.

Jade Emperor: Was Queen Mother of the West correct, my dear daughter?

Sister Moon: Oh, yes, it was wonderful! I'll always wear my veil, and I'll keep watch over the people at night for as long as Sister Sun warms the days! I won't even miss my polished jewelry . . . not much, anyway.

Jade Emperor: And I will send a helper—the Heavenly Bear—to be your guard and walk in a circle around your coach as you travel, my daughter.

Sister Moon: But won't the Heavenly Bear block some of my light?

Jade Emperor: Yes, that is exactly my plan! As he moves slowly in front of you, your light will be dimmed a little each day, until he is entirely blocking you from the view of the people. Then as he moves farther around your coach, you will become brighter each night until finally he is behind you, and the people can see your full face. In this way, you will show the people the passage of time.

Queen Mother of the West: As Sister Sun lets the people know the change of the seasons, you will help them follow time from day to day, week to week, and month to month.

Sister Moon: This is the happiest moment of my life! I can't wait for the day to end so that I can cross the night sky again!

Narrator: And that is why the moon is ivory and why the nights always seem brightest during the winter months, when the days are short and the nights are long. Sister Moon is happiest then because she gets to spend more time doing what she loves best—watching over the people of Earth.